Book 1
Python Programming In A Day

BY SAM KEY

&

Book 2
CSS Programming Professional Made Easy

BY SAM KEY

Book 1
Python Programming In A Day

BY SAM KEY

Beginners Power Guide To Learning Python Programming From Scratch

Programming Box Set #40: Python Programming in a Day & CSS Programming Professional Made Easy

Table Of Contents

Introduction

I want to thank you and congratulate you for purchasing the book, "Python Programming in a Day: Beginners Power Guide To Learning Python Programming From Scratch".

This book contains proven steps and strategies on how you can program using Python in a day or less. It will contain basic information about the programming language. And let you familiarize with programming overall.

Python is one of the easiest and most versatile programming languages today. Also, it is a powerful programming language that is being used by expert developers on their complex computer programs. And its biggest edges against other programming languages are its elegant but simple syntax and readiness for rapid application development.

With python, you can create standalone programs with complex functionalities. In addition, you can combine it or use it as an extension language for programs that were created using other programming languages.

Anyway, this eBook will provide you with easy and understandable tutorial about python. It will only cover the basics of the programming language. On the other hand, the book is a good introduction to some basic concept of programming. It will be not too technical, and it is focused on teaching those who have little knowledge about the craft of developing programs.

By the way, take note that this tutorial will use python 3.4.2. Also, most of the things mentioned here are done in a computer running on Microsoft Windows.

Thanks again for purchasing this book. I hope you enjoy it!

Chapter 1: Getting Prepared

In developing python scripts or programs, you will need a text editor. It is recommended that you use Notepad++. It is a free and open source text editor that you can easily download and install from the internet. For you to have the latest version, go to this link: http://notepad-plus-plus.org/download/v6.6.9.html.

Once you install Notepad++ and you are ready to write python code lines, make sure that you take advantage of its syntax-highlighting feature. To do that, click on Language > P > Python. All python functions will be automatically highlighted when you set the Language to python. It will also highlight strings, numbers, etc. Also, if you save the file for the first time, the save dialog box will automatically set the file to have an extension of .py.

To be able to run your scripts, download and install python into your computer. The latest version, as of this writing, is 3.4.2. You can get python from this link: https://www.python.org/download.

And to be able to test run your python scripts in Notepad++, go to Run > Run... or press the F5 key. A small dialogue box will appear, and it will require you to provide the path for the compiler or a program that will execute your script. In this case, you will need to direct Notepad++ to the python executable located in the installation folder.

By default or if you did not change the installation path of python, it can be found on the root folder on the drive where your operating system is installed. If your operating system is on drive C of your computer, the python executable can be found on C:\Python34\python.exe. Paste that line on the dialogue box and add the following line: $(FULL_CURRENT_PATH). Separate the location of the python.exe and the line with a space, and enclosed the latter in double quotes. It should look like this:

C:\Python34\python.exe "$(FULL_CURRENT_PATH)"

Save this setting by pressing the Save button in the dialogue box. Another window will popup. It will ask you to name the setting and assign a shortcut key to it. Just name it python34 and set the shortcut key to F9. Press the OK button and close the dialogue box. With that setting, you can test run your program by just pressing the F9 key.

By the way, if the location you have set is wrong, the python executable will not run. So to make sure you got it right, go to python folder. And since you are already there, copy python.exe, and paste its shortcut on your desktop. You will need to access it later.

And you are all set. You can proceed on learning python now.

Chapter 2: Interactive Mode – Mathematical Operations

Before you develop multiple lines of code for a program, it will be best for you to start playing around with Python's interactive mode first. The interactive mode allows a developer to see immediate results of what he will code in his program. For new python users, it can help them familiarize themselves on python's basic functions, commands, and syntax.

To access the interactive mode, just open python.exe. If you followed the instructions in the previous chapter, its shortcut should be already on your desktop. Just open it and the python console will appear.

Once you open the python executable, a command console like window will appear. It will greet you with a short message that will tell you the version of python that you are using and some command that can provide you with various information about python. At the bottom of the message, you will the primary prompt (>>>). Beside that is the blinking cursor. In there, you can just type the functions or commands you want to use or execute. For starters, type credits and press Enter.

Mathematical Operations in Interactive Mode

You can actually use the interactive mode as a calculator. Try typing 1 + 1 and press Enter. Immediately after you press the Enter, the console provided you with the answer to the equation 1 + 1. And then it created a new line and the primary prompt is back.

In python, there are eight basic mathematical operations that you can execute. And they are:

- Addition = 1 + 1

- Subtraction = 1 – 1

- Multiplication = 1 * 1

- Division = 1 / 1

In older versions of Python, if you divide integers and the division will result to a decimal, Python will only return an integer. For example, if you divide 3 by 2, you will get 1 as an answer. And if you divide 20 by 39, you will get a zero. Also, take note that the result is not rounded off. Python will just truncate all numbers after the decimal point.

In case you want to get an accurate quotient with decimals, you must convert the integers into floating numbers. To do that, you can simply add a decimal point after the numbers.

- Floor Division = 1 // 1

If you are dividing floating numbers and you just want to get the integer quotient or you do not want the decimals to be included, you can perform floor division instead. For example, floor dividing 5.1515 by 2.0 will give you a 2 as an integer quotient.

- Modulo = 1 % 1

The modulo operator will allow you to get the remainder from a division from two numbers. For example, typing 5 % 2 will give you a result of 1 since 5 divided by two is 2 remainder 1.

- Negation = -1

Adding a hyphen before a number will make it a negative number. You can perform double, triple, or multiple negations with this operator. For example, typing -23 will result into -23. Typing --23 will result into 23. Typing -----23 will result into -23.

- Absolute Value = abs(1)

When this is used to a number, the number will be converted to its absolute value or will be always positive. For example, abs (-41) will return 41.

Python calculates equation using the PEMDAS order, the order of operations that are taught in Basic Math, Geometry, and Algebra subjects in schools. By the way, PEMDAS stands for Parentheses, Exponents, Multiplication, Division, Addition, and Subtraction.

Chapter 3: Interactive Mode – Variables

During your Math subject when you were in grade or high school, your teacher might have taught you about variables. In Math, variables are letters that serve as containers for numbers of known and unknown value. In Python or any programming language, variables are important. They act as storage of values. And their presence makes the lives of developers easy.

However, unlike in school, variables in programming languages are flexible when it comes to their names and functions. In Python, variables can have names instead of a single letter. Also, they can also contain or represent text or strings.

Assigning Values to Variables

Assigning a value to a variable is easy in Python. You can just type the name of your variable, place an equal sign afterwards, and place the value you want to be contained or stored in the variable. For example:

```
>>> x = 151
```

When you assign a value in a variable, Python will not reply any message. Instead, it will just put your cursor on the next primary prompt. In the example, you have assigned the value 151 to the variable x. To check if it worked, type x on the console and press Enter. Python will respond with the value of the variable x.

Just like numbers, you can perform arithmetical operations with variable. For example, try typing $x - 100$ in the console and press Enter. Python will calculate the equation, and return the number 51 since $151 - 100 = 51$. And of course, you can perform mathematical operations with multiple variables in one line.

By the way, in case that you did not define or assign a value to a new variable, Python will return an error if you use it. For example, if you try to subtract x with y, you will get an error that will say name 'y' is not defined. You received that message since you have not assigned anything to the variable y yet.

In addition, you can assign and change the value of a variable anytime. Also, the variable's value will not change if you do not assign anything to it. The variable and its value will stay in your program as long as you do not destroy it, delete it, or close the program.

To delete a variable, type del then the name of the variable. For example:

>>> del x

Once you try to access the variable again by typing its name and pressing Enter after you delete it, Python will return an error message saying that the variable is not defined.

Also, you can assign calculated values to a variable. For example:

>>> z = 1 + 4

If you type that, type z, and press Enter, Python will reply with 5. Variables are that easy to manipulate in Python.

You can also assign the value of one variable to another. Below is an example:

>>> y = 2

>>> z = y

The variable z's value will be changed to 2.

Chapter 4: Interactive Mode – Strings

Your program will not be all about numbers. Of course, you would want to add some text into it. In Python, you can do that by using strings. A string or string literal is a series of alphanumeric numbers or characters. A string can be a word or sentence. A lone character can be also considered as a string. To make your program display a string, you will need to use the print function. Below is an example on how to use it:

>>> print ("Dogs are cute.")

To display a string using the print function properly, you will need to enclose the string with parentheses and double quotations. Without the parentheses, you will receive a syntax error. Without the quotes, Python will think that you are trying to make it display a variable's value.

By the way, in older versions of Python, you can use print without the parentheses. However, in version 3 and newer, print was changed to as a function. Because of that, it will require parentheses.

For example:

>>> print ("Dogs")

That line will make Python print the word or string Dogs. On the other hand:

>>> print (Dogs)

That line will return a variable not defined error. With that being said, you can actually print or display the content of a variable. For example:

>>> x = 14

>>> print (x)

The print function will display the number 14 on the screen. By the way, you can also use single quotes or even triple single or double quotes. However, it is recommendable to use a single double for those who are just started in program development.

Assigning Strings to Variables

Assigning strings to variables is easy. And it is the same as assigning numbers to them. The only difference is that you will need to enclose the string value in double quotations or reverse commas as some developers call them. For example:

>>> stringvariable = "This is a string."

If you type stringvariable in the interactive mode console, it will display the This is a string text. On the other hand, if you do this:

>>> print (stringvariable)

Python will print the string, too.

Strings can include punctuation and symbols. However, there are some symbols or punctuations that can mess up your assignment and give you a syntax error. For example:

>>> samplestring = "And he said, "Hi.""

In this case, you will get a syntax error because the appearance of another double quote has appeared before the double quote that should be enclosing the string. Unfortunately, Python cannot recognize what you are trying to do here. Because of that, you need the by escaping the string literal.

To escape, you must place the escape character backslash (\) before the character that might produce conflict. In the example's case, the characters that might produce a syntax error are the two double quotes inside. Below is the fixed version of the previous paragraph:

>>> samplestring = "And he said, \"Hi.\""

Writing the string assignment like that will not produce an error. In case you print or type and enter the variable samplestring in the console, you will see the string that you want to appear, which is And he said, "Hi.".

Escape Sequences in Python

Not all characters are needed to be escaped. Due to that, the characters that you can escape or the number of escape sequences are limited. Also, escape sequences are not only for preventing syntax errors. They are also used to add special characters such as new line and carriage return to your strings. Below is a list of the escape sequences you can use in Python:

- \\ = Backslash (\)

- \" = Double quote (")

- \' = Single quote (')

- \b = Backspace

- \a = ASCII Bell

- \n = Linefeed

- \f = Formfeed

- \t = Horizontal Tab

- \r = Carriage Return

- \v = ASCII Vertical Tab

Preventing Escape Sequences to Work

There will be times that the string that you want to print or use might accidentally contain an escape sequence. Though, it is a bit rare since the backslash character is seldom used in everyday text. Nevertheless, it is still best that you know how to prevent it. Below is an example of an escape sequence that might produce undesirable results to your program:

>>> print ("C:\Windows\notepad.exe")

When Python processes that, you might encounter a problem when you use since the \n in the middle of the string will break the string. For you to visualize it better, below is the result:

>>> print ("C:\Windows\notepad.exe")

C:\Windows

otepad.exe

>>> _

To prevent that you must convert your string to a raw string. You can do that by placing the letter r before the string that you will print. Below is an example:

>>> print (r"C:\Windows\notepad.exe")

C:\Windows\notepad.exe

>>> _

Basic String Operations

In Python, you can perform operations on your strings. These basic string operations also use the common arithmetical operators, but when those operators are used on strings, they will produce different results. There are two of these. And they use the + and * operators. Below are examples on how to use them:

>>> print ("cat" + "dog")

catdog

>>> print ("cat" * 3)

catcatcat

>>> _

When the + operator is used between two strings, it will combine them. On the other hand, if the multiplication operator is used, the string will be repeated depending on the number indicated.

By the way, you cannot use operators between strings and numbers – with the exception of the multiplication symbol. For example:

```
>>> variable_x = 1 + "text"
```

The example above will return an unsupported operand type since Python does not know what to do when you add a string and a number.

Chapter 5: Transition from Interactive Mode to Programming Mode

Alright, by this time, you must already have a good feel on Python's interactive mode. You also know the basic concepts of variables, strings, and numbers. Now, it is time to put them together and create a simple program.

You can now close Python's window and open Notepad++. A new file should be currently opened once you open that program. The next step is to set the Language setting into Python. And save the file. Any name will do as long that you make sure that your file's extension is set to .py or Python file. In case the save function does not work, type anything on the text file. After you save it, remove the text you typed.

Now, you will start getting used to programming mode. Programming mode is where program development start. Unlike interactive mode, programming mode requires you to code first, save your file, and run it on Python. To get a feel of the programming mode, copy this sample below:

print ("Hello World!")

print ("This is a simple program that aims to display text.")

print ("That is all.")

input ("Press Enter Key to End this Program")

If you followed the instructions on the Getting Prepared chapter, press the F9 key. Once you do, Python will run and execute your script. It will be read line by line by Python just like in Interactive mode. The only difference is that the primary prompt is not there, and you cannot input any command while it is running.

Input Function

On the other hand, the example code uses the input function. The input function's purpose is to retrieve any text that the user will type in the program and wait for the Enter key to be pressed before going to the next line of code below it. And when the user presses the key the program will close since there are no remaining lines of code to execute.

By the way, if you remove the input function from the example, the program will just print the messages in it and close itself. And since Python will process those lines within split seconds, you will be unable to see if it work. So, in the following examples and lessons, the input function will be used to temporarily pause your scripts or prevent your program to close prematurely.

You can use the input function to assign values to variables. Check this example out:

```
print ( "Can you tell me your name?" )

name = input("Please type your name: ")

print ( "Your name is " + name + "." )

print ( "That is all." )

input ( "Press Enter Key to End this Program. \n" )
```

In this example, the variable name was assigned a value that will come from user input through the input function. When you run it, the program will pause on the Please type your name part and wait for user input. The user can place almost anything on it. And when he presses enter, Python will capture the text, and store it to variable name.

Once the name is established, the print function will confirm it and mention the content of the name variable.

Data Type Conversion

You can also use the input function to get numbers. However, to make sure the program will understand that its numbers that it will receive, make sure that your input does not include non-numeric characters. Below is a sample code of an adding program:

```
print ( "This program will add two numbers you would input." )

first_number = input ( "Type the first number: " )

second_number = input ( "Type the second number: " )

sum = int(first_number) + int(second_number)

print ( "The sum is " + str(sum) )

input ( "Press Enter Key to End this Program. \n" )
```

In this example, the program tries to get numbers from the user. And get the sum of those two numbers. However, there is a problem. The input function only produces string data. That means that even if you type in a number, the input will still assign a string version of that number to the variable.

And since they are both strings, you cannot add them as numbers. And if you do add them, it will result into a joined string. For example, if the first number was 1 and the second number was 2, the sum that will appear will be 12, which is mathematically wrong.

In order to fix that, you will need to convert the strings into its numeric form. In this example, they will be converted to integers. With the help of the int function, that can be easily done. Any variable will be converted to integer when placed inside the int function.

So, to get the integer sum of the first_number and second_number, both of them were converted into integers. By the way, converting only one of them will result into an error. With that done, the sum of the two numbers will be correctly produced, which 3.

Now the second roadblock is the print function. In the last print function, the example used an addition operator to join the The sum is text and the variable sum. However, since the variable sum is an integer, the operation will return an error. Just like before, you should convert the variable in order for the operation to work. In this case, the sum variable was converted to a string using the str function.

There are other data types in Python – just like with other programming languages. This part will not cover the technicalities of those data types and about the memory allocation given to them, but this part is to just familiarize you with it. Nevertheless, below is a list of a few of the data type conversion functions you might use while programming in Python:

- Long() – converts data to a long integer

- Hex() – converts integers to hexadecimal

- Float() – converts data to floating-point

- Unichr() – converts integers to Unicode

- Chr() – converts integers to characters

- Oct() – converts integers to octal

Chapter 6: Programming Mode – Conditional Statements

Just displaying text and getting text from user are not enough for you to make a decent program out of Python. You need your program to be capable of interacting with your user and be capable of producing results according to their inputs.

Because of that, you will need to use conditional statements. Conditional statements allow your program to execute code blocks according to the conditions you set. For you to get more familiar with conditional statements, check the example below:

```
print ( "Welcome to Guess the Number Game! " )

magic_number = input ( "Type your guess: " )

if ( magic_number  == "1" ):

   print ( "You Win!" )

else:

   print ( "You Lose!" )

input ( "Press enter to exit this program " )
```

In this example, the if or conditional statement is used. The syntax of this function differs a bit from the other functions discussed earlier. In this one, you will need to set a conditional argument on its parentheses. The condition is that if the variable magic_number is equal to 1, then the code block under it will run. The colon after the condition indicates that it will have a code block beneath it.

When you go insert a code block under a statement, you will need to indent them. The code block under the if statement is print ("You Win!"). Because of that, it is and should be indented. If the condition is satisfied, which will happen if the user entered 1, then the code block under if will run. If the condition was not satisfied,

it will be ignored, and Python will parse on the next line with the same indent
level as if.

That next line will be the else statement. If and else go hand in hand. The have
identical function. If their conditions are satisfied, then the program will run the
code block underneath them. However, unlike if, else has a preset condition. Its
condition is that whenever the previous conditional statement is not satisfied,
then it will run its code block. And that also means that if the previous
conditional statement's condition was satisfied, it will not run.

Due to that, if the user guesses the right magic number, then the code block of if
will run and the else statement's code block will be ignored. If the user was
unable to guess the right magic number, if's code block will be ignored and else's
code block will run.

Conclusion

Thank you again for purchasing this book!

I hope this book was able to help you to understand the basic concepts of programming and become familiar in Python in just one day.

The next step is to research and learn looping in Python. Loops are control structures that can allow your program to repeat various code blocks. They are very similar to conditional statements. The only difference is that, their primary function is to repeat all the lines of codes placed inside their codeblocks. Also, whenever the parser of Python reaches the end of its code block, it will go back to the loop statement and see if the condition is still satisfied. In case that it is, it will loop again. In case that it does not, it will skip its code block and move to the next line with the same indent level.

In programming, loops are essential. Truth be told, loops compose most functionalities of complex programs. Also, when it comes to coding efficiency, loops makes program shorter and faster to develop. Using loops in your programs will reduce the size of your codes. And it will reduce the amount of time you need to write all the codes you need to achieve the function you desire in your program.

If you do not use loops in your programs, you will need to repeat typing or pasting lines of codes that might span to hundreds of instances – whereas if you use loops in your programs, those hundred instances can be reduced into five or seven lines of codes.

There are multiple methods on how you can create a loop in your program. Each loop method or function has their unique purposes. Trying to imitate another loop method with one loop method can be painstaking.

On the other hand, once you are done with loops, you will need to upgrade your current basic knowledge about Python. Research about all the other operators that were not mentioned in this book, the other data types and their quirks and functions, simple statements, compound statements, and top-level components.

To be honest, Python is huge. You have just seen a small part of it. And once you delve deeper on its other capabilities and the possible things you could create with it, you will surely get addicted to programming.

Finally, if you enjoyed this book, please take the time to share your thoughts and post a review on Amazon. We do our best to reach out to readers and provide the best value we can. Your positive review will help us achieve that. It'd be greatly appreciated!

Thank you and good luck!

Book 2
CSS Programming Professional Made Easy

By Sam Key

Expert CSS Programming Language Success in a Day for any Computer User!

Programming Box Set #40: Python Programming in a Day & CSS Programming Professional Made Easy

Table of Contents

Introduction

I want to thank you and congratulate you for purchasing the book, "Professional CSS Programming Made Easy: Expert CSS Programming Language Success In A Day for any Computer User!".

This book contains proven steps and strategies on how to effectively apply CSS style rules in making your webpages more appealing to your readers. In this book, the different aspects of CSS programming are discussed in simple language to make it easy for you to understand even if you have no previous experience in programming. In no time, you can start creating your own CSS style rules!

Thanks again for purchasing this book, I hope you enjoy it!

Chapter 1: What is CSS?

CSS is short for Cascading Style Sheets which is a simple design language that is meant to streamline the enhancement of web page presentations. Basically, through CSS, you will be able to manage how a web page looks and feels. When you use CSS, you will be able to control the background color or image in the web page, the color of the texts, the style of the font, the size of the columns, the column layout, the spacing in between paragraphs and a whole lot more of design effects.

Even though CSS is quite simple to understand, it can provide you with great control of how an HTML document is presented. People who study CSS often study other markup languages such as XHTML or HTML.

What are the advantages of CSS?

- CSS will allow you to save time. After you have written a CSS code once, you can then use the same sheet in various web pages. You can create a style for each web page element and then use it to as many HTML pages as you desire in the future.

- Your web pages will load faster. If you will use CSS in your web pages, you no longer have to write an HTML tag attribute all the time. You simple create 1 CSS rule of a tag and then use it for all the incidences of that specific tag. When you use less HTML codes, it translates to faster download speed.

- Your web pages become easier to maintain. If you wish to create a global change in your website, all you need to do is adjust the style and then all the elements included in your different web pages will be automatically adjusted.

- You will be able to enjoy better styles compared to HTML. The style attributes available for HTML codes are lesser compared to what you can work with when you use CSS. This means that you will be able to create top quality styles for your web pages.

- You will have multiple device compatibility. With CSS, you will be allowed to use content that can be optimized for different types of device. Even when you use the same HTML document, you can present the website in various versions for different devices such as mobile phones, tablets, desktop and even printing.

- You will be able to adopt web standards that are recognized globally. More and more people are losing interest in using HTML attributes and have started to recommend the use of CSS.

- You get to future-proof. By using CSS in your web pages now, you can also ensure that they will have compatibility with future browsers.

Creation and Maintenance of CSS

Only a small group of people within the World Wide Web Consortium (W3C) referred to as the CSS Working Group is allowed to create and maintain CSS. This group generates the CSS specifications which are then submitted to the W3C members for discussion and ratification. Only ratified specifications are given the recommendation signal by the W3C. You need to note that they are referred to as recommendations since the W3C cannot really dictate how the language is to be actually implementation. The software the implement the CSS language is created by independent organizations and companies.

Note: If you wish to know, yes, the W3C is the group that provides the recommendations on how the Internet should work and how it should progress.

Different CSS Versions

The W3C released CSS1 or Cascading Style Sheets Level 1was released as a recommendation in 1996. The recommendation included a description of the CSS together with a basic visual formatting model that can be used for every HTML tag.

In May 1998, the W3C released the recommendation for CSS2 or Cascading Style Sheets Level 2 which included further information that builds on CSS1. CSS2 added support for style sheets for specific media such as aural devices, printers, element tables and positioning and downloadable fonts.

Chapter 2: Various Types of CSS Selectors

A CSS is composed of different style rules that are translated by the browser for them to be applied to the specific elements in your web page. A style rule is further composed of 3 parts: selector, property and value. A selector is the HTML tag wherein the style rule will be applied. Examples include <table> or <h1>. A property is the specific attribute type that an HTML tag has. In simple terms, you could say that each HTML attribute is ultimately translated to a CSS property. Examples of properties include border or color. Values, on the other hand, are directly assigned to the properties. For instance, for the color property, you can assign a value of #000000 or black.

One way to write a CSS Style Rule Syntax is: Selector (property: value)

Ex. You can write the syntax rule for a table border as: table (border: 2px solid #C00;). The selector in this example is table while the property is the border. The specific value given for the property is 2px solid #C00.

In this chapter, we will be talking about the different kinds of selectors.

Type Selector

The selector in the example given above (table) is categorized under the Type Selector. Another example of a type Selector is "level 1 heading" or "h1). We can write a CSS Style Rule Syntax as: h1 (color: #36CFFF;). The selector in this example is h1 while the property is the color. The specific value given for the property is #36CFFF.

Universal Selector

This is designated by an asterisk (*) which means that the style rule syntax that you want to create will be applied to all elements in your webpage and not only to specific elements.

Example: *(color: #FFFFFF;). This style rule means that you want all of the elements (including fonts, borders, etc.) in your webpage to be white.

Descendant Selector

You use the descendant selector when you wish to apply a certain style rule for a specific element that lies within a specific element.

Example: ul em (color:#FFFFFF;), the value #FFFFFF (white) will only be applied to the property (color) if the selector/property <em> lies within the selector <ul>.

Class Selector

Using the Class Selector, you will be able to define a specific style rule that can be applied based on the specific class attribute of elements. This means that all of the elements that have that specific class attributed will have the same formatting as specified in the style rule.

Example 1: .white (color: #FFFFFF;). Here the class attribute is "white" and it means that the color "white" will be applied to all of the elements given the class attribute "white" in your document.

Example 2: h1.white (color: #FFFFFF;). This style rule is more specific. The class attribute is still "white" and the style rule will be applied to the elements given the class attribute "white" but ONLY if they are ALSO an <h1> or "level 1 heading" element.

You can actually give one or more class selectors for each element. For example, you can give the class selectors "center" and "bold" to a paragraph <p> by writing it as <p class="center,bold">.

ID Selector

You use an ID selector to create a style rule that is based on the specific ID attribute of the element. This means that all of the elements that have that specific ID will have the same format as defined in the style rule.

Example 1: #white (color: #FFFFFF;). The ID assigned here is "white" and the style rule means that all elements with the "white" ID attribute will be rendered black in your document.

Example 2: h1#white (color: #FFFFFF;). This is more specific because it means that the style rule will only be applied to elements with the ID attribute "white" ONLY IF they are a level 1 heading element.

The ID selectors are ideally used as foundations for descendant selectors. Example: #white h3 (color: #FFFFFF;). The style rule dictates that all level 3 headings located in the different pages of your website will be displayed in white color ONLY IF those level 3 headings are within tags that have an ID attribute of "white".

Child Selector

The Child Selector is quite similar to the Descendant Selector except that they have different functionalities.

Example: body > p (color: #FFFFFF;). The style rule states that a paragraph will be rendered in white if it is a direct child of the <body> element. If the paragraph is within other elements such as <td> or <div>, the style rule will not apply to it.

Attribute Selector

You can apply specific styles to your webpage elements that have specific attributes.

Example: input(type="text"](color: #FFFFFF;).

One benefit of the above example is that the specified color in the style rule will only affect your desired text field and will not affect the <input type="submit"/>.

You need to keep the following rules in mind when using attribute selectors:

• p[lang]. All elements of the paragraph that has a "lang" attribute will be selected.

• p[lang="fr"]. All elements of the paragraph that has a "lang" attribute AND the value "fr" in the "lang" attribute will be selected. Note that the value should exactly be "fr".

• p[lang~="fr"]. All elements of the paragraph that has a "lang" attribute AND CONTAINS the value "fr" in the "lang" attribute will be selected.

• p[lang |="ne"]. All elements of the paragraph that has a "lang" attribute AND CONTAINS value that is EITHER exactly "en" or starts with "en-" in the "lang" attribute will be selected.

Multiple Style Rules

It is possible for you to create multiple style rules for one specific element. The style rules can be defined in such a way that different properties are combined into a single block and specific values are assigned to each property.

Example 1:

h1(color: #35C; font-weight: bold; letter-spacing: .5em; margin-bottom: 1em; text-transform: uppercase;)

You will note that the properties and their corresponding values are separated from other property/value pairs by using a semi-colon. You can opt to write the combine style rules as a single line similar to the example above or as multiple lines for better readability. The example below is just the same as Example 1:

Example 2:

h1 (

color: #35C;

font-weight: bold;

letter-spacing: .5em;

margin-bottom: 1em;

text-transform: uppercase;

)

How to Group Selectors

You can actually apply one single style to different selectors. All you really need to do is write all the selectors at the start of your style rule but make sure that they are separated by a comma. The examples above both pertain to the selector or property "level 1 heading". If you want to apply the same style rule to "level 2 heading" and "level 3 heading", you can include h2 and h3 in the first line, as follows:

Example:

h1, h2, h3 (

color: #35C;

font-weight: bold;

letter-spacing: .5em;

margin-bottom: 1em;

text-transform: uppercase;

)

Note that the sequence of the selector element is not relevant. You can write it as h3,h2,h1 and the style rule will exactly be the same. It means that the specified style rules will still be applied to all the elements of the selectors.

It is also possible to create a style rule that combines different class selectors.

Example:

#supplement, #footer, #content (

position: absolute;

left: 520px;

width: 210px;

)

Chapter 3: Methods of Associating Styles

There are actually 4 methods of associating styles within an HTML document – Embedded CSS, Inline CSS, External CSS and Imported CSS. But the two most frequently used are Inline CSS and External CSS.

Embedded CSS

This method uses the <style> element wherein the tags are positioned within the <head>...</head> tags. All elements that exist within your document will be affected by a rule that has been written using this syntax. The generic syntax is as follows:

<head>

<style type="text/css" media=". . .">

Style Rules

. . . .

</style>

</head>

The following attributes that are connected to the <style> element are as follows:

•   Type with value "text/css". This attribute indicates the style sheet language as a content-type (MIME type). You need to note that this attribute is always required.

•   Media with values as "screen", "tty", "tv", "projection", "handheld", "print", "braille", "aural" or "all". This attribute indicates what kind of device the webpage will be shown. This attribute is only optional and it always has "all" as a default value.

 Example:

<head>

<style type="text/css" media="screen">

h2(

color: #38C;

)

</style>

</head>

Inline CSS

This method uses the style attribute of a specific HTML element in defining the style rule. This means that the style rule will only be applied to the specific HTML element ONLY. The generic syntax is as follows: <element style=". . .style rules. . . .">

Only one attribute is connected to the <style> attribute and it is as follows:

•   Style with value "style rules". The value that you will specify for the style attribute is basically a combination of various style declarations. You should use a semicolon to separate the different style declarations.

Example:

<h2 style ="color:#000;">. This is inline CSS </h2>

External CSS

This method uses the <link> element in defining the style rule. You can use it to add external style sheets within your webpage. The external style sheet that you will add will have a different text file that has the extension .css. All the style rules that you want to apply to your webpage elements will be added inside the external text file and then you can append the text file in any of your web pages by creating the <link> element. The general syntax that you will be using will be:

<head>

<link type="text/css" href=" . . ." media=" . . ." />

</head>

The following attributes that are connected with the <style> elements are as follows:

•   Type with the value "text/css". This indicates that you are using a MIME type or a content type for your style sheet language. Note that you are always required to use this attribute.

•   Href with value "URL". This attribute will indicate the specific style sheet file that contains your style rules. Again, you are also always required to use this attribute.

• Media with value "screen", "tty", "tv", "projection", "handheld", "print", "braille", "aural" or "all". This attribute indicates the specific media device that you will use to display the document. This attribute is only optional and it has a default value of "all".

Example wherein the style sheet file is named as docstyle.css:

h2, h3 (

color: #38C;

font-weight: bold;

letter-spacing: .5em;

margin-bottom: 2em;

text-transform: uppercase;

)

Then you can add your style sheet file "docstyle.css" in your webpage by adding these rules:

<head>

<link type="text/css" href="docstyle.css" media="all" />

</head>

Imported CSS

This method which uses the @import rule is the same as the <link> element because it is used to import an external style sheet file to your webpage. The generic syntax of this method is as follows:

<head>

<@import "URL";

</head>

Here is another alternative syntax that you can use:

<head>

<@import url ("URL");

</head>

Example:

<head>

@import "docstyle.css'"

</head>

How to Override CSS Style Rules

The following can override the style rules that you have created using the above four methods:

• An inline style sheet is given the number one priority. This means that an inline style sheet will always supersede a rule that has been written with a <style>...</style> tag or a rule that has been defined in an external stylesheet file.

• A rule that has been written with a <style>...</style> tag will always supersede a style rule that has been defined in an external stylesheet file.

• The rules that you define within an external stylesheet file is always given the lowest priority. This means that any rules defined within the external file will only be applied if the 2 rules above aren't valid.

How to Handle an Old Browser:

Currently, there are a lot of old browsers that are not yet capable of supporting CSS. When you are working with these kind of browsers, you need to write your embedded CSS within the HTML document. Here is an example on how you can embed CSS in an old browser:

<style type="text/css">

<!—

Body, td (

   Color: red;

)

-->

</style>

How to Add a CSS Comment

In case it is necessary for you to include an additional comment within the style sheet block, you can easily do this by writing your comment within /*....this is a comment in style sheet....*/.   The /*....*/ method used in C++ and C programming languages can also be used in adding comments in a multi-line block.

Example:

/* This is an external style sheet file */

h3, h2, h1 (

color: #38C;

font-weight: bold;

letter-spacing: .5em;

margin-bottom: 2em;

text-transform: uppercase;

)

/* end of style rules. */

Chapter 4: Measurement Units

There are several measurements that CSS can support. These include absolute units like inch, centimeter, points, etc. They also include relative measures like em unit and percentage. These values are important when you want to specify the different measurements you want to include in your style rule. Example:

border="2px solid black".

Here are the most common measurements that you will use in creating CSS style rules:

Unit of Measure	Description	Example
%	Indicates measurements as a percentage in relation to another value which is normally an enclosing element	p {font-size: 12pt; line-height: 150%;}
cm	Indicates measurements in centimeter	div {margin-bottom: 1.5cm;}
em	A relative number used in measuring font height using em spaces. One em unit is equal to the size of a particular font. This means, if you want a certain font to have a size of 10pt, one "em" unit is equal to 10pt and 3em is equal to 30pt.	p {letter-spacing: 6em;}
ex	A number used to define a measurement in relation to the x-height of a font. The x-height is defined by the height of letter x in lowercase in any given font.	p {font-size: 20pt: line-height: 2ex;}
in	Indicates measurements in inches	p {word-spacing: .12in;}
mm	Indicates measurements in millimeter	p {word-spacing: 12mm;}
pc	Indicates measurements in picas. One pica is equal to 12 points. This	p {font-size: 18pc;}

	means that there are six picas in one inch.	
pt	Indicates measurements in points. One point is equal to 1/72 of one inch.	body {font-size: 20pt;}
px	Indicates measurements in screen pixel	p {padding: 32px;}

Chapter 5: Style Rules Using Colors

A color in CSS style rules is indicated by color values. Normally, the color values are used to define the color of either the background of an element or its foreground (that is, its text). You can also utilize colors to change how your borders and other aesthetic effects look.

Color values in CSS rules can be specified using the following formats:

•   Hex code using the syntax #RRGGBB. Example: p {color: #FFFF00;}. The six digits represent one specific color wherein RR represents the value for red, GG the value for green and BB the value for blue. You can get the hexadecimal values of different colors from graphics software such as Jasc Paintshop Pro and Adobe Photoshop. You can also use the Advanced Paint Brush to get the hexadecimal values. You need to note that the six digits should always be preceded by the hash or pound sign (#).

•   Short hex code using the syntax #RGB. Example: p {color: #7A6;}. This is the shorter version of the hexadecimal value. You can also get them from Jasc Paintshop Pro, Adobe Photoshop or Advanced Paint Brush.

•   RGB % using the syntax rgb (rrr%, ggg%, bbb%). Example: p{color: rgb (40%, 50%, 40%);}. This format is actually advisable to use because not all browsers support this type of format.

•   RGB Absolute using the syntax rgb (rrr,ggg, bbb). Example: p {color: rgb (255,0,0);}

•   Keyword using the syntax black, aqua, etc. Example: p {color: red;}

Chapter 6: How to Set Backgrounds

What you will learn in this chapter includes how to define the background of the different elements in your web page. You can use any of the following background properties for specific elements in your webpage:

•   You can use the background color property to define the background color of your element.

•   You can use the background image property to define the background image of your element.

•   You can use the background repeat property to control whether your background image will be repeated or not.

•   You can use the background position property to control the position of the background image.

•   You can use the background attachment property to define whether your image is fixed or will scroll with the rest of the webpage.

•   You can use the background property to combine the above properties into one style rule.

Background Color

Here is a sample of how you can define the background color:

RED

This will result in RED.

Background Image

Here is a sample of how you can define the background image:

<table style="background-image:url (/images/pattern1.jpg);">

<tr><td>

The table now has an image in the background.

</td></tr>

</table>

How to Repeat a Background Image

In case your image is small, you can opt to repeat your background image. Otherwise, you can simple utilize the "no-repeat" value in the background-repeat property if you do not wish to have your background image repeated. This means that your image will only be displayed once. Note that "repeat value" is the default value in the background-repeat property.

Example:

<table style="background-image:url (/images/pattern2.jpg);

        background-repeat: repeat;">

<tr><td>

The background image in this table will be repeated several times.

</td></tr>

</table>

Here is a sample rule if you want the background image to be repeated vertically:

<table style="background-image:url (/images/pattern2.jpg);

        background-repeat: repeat-y;">

<tr><td>

The background image in this table will be repeated vertically.

</td></tr>

</table>

Here is a sample rule if you want the background image to be repeated horizontally:

<table style="background-image:url (/images/pattern2.jpg);

        background-repeat: repeat-x;">

\<tr>\<td>

The background image in this table will be repeated horizontally.

\</td>\</tr>

\</table>

How to Set the Position of the Background Image

Here is a sample of how you can define the position of a background image at 150 pixels from the left side:

\<table style="background-image: url (/images/pattern2.jpg);

Background-position:150px;">

\<tr>\<td>

The position of the background is now 150 pixels from the left side.

\</td>\</tr>

\</table>

Here is a sample of how you can define the position of a background image at 300 pixels from the top and 150 pixels from the left side:

\<table style="background-image: url (/images/pattern2.jpg);

Background-position:150px 300px;">

\<tr>\<td>

The position of the background is now 300 pixels from the top and 150 pixels from the left side.

\</td>\</tr>

\</table>

How to Define the Background Attachment

The background attachment indicates whether the background image that you have set is fixed in its place or scrolls when you move the webpage.

Here is an example on how to write a style rule with a background image that is fixed:

<p style="background-image:url (/images/pattern2.jpg);

   Background-attachment:fixed;">

The paragraph now has a background image that is fixed.

</p>

Here is an example on how to write a style rule with a background image that scrolls with the webpage:

<p style="background-image:url (/images/pattern2.jpg);

   Background-attachment:scroll;">

The paragraph now has a background image that scrolls with the webpage.

</p>

How to Use the Shorthand Property

You can actually utilize the background property in order to define all of the background properties all at the same time.

Example:

<p style="background:url (/images/pattern2.jpg) repeat scroll;">

The background image of this paragraph has a scroll and repeated properties.

</p>

Chapter 7: How to Set Font Properties

What you will learn in this chapter includes how to define the following font properties to a specific element in your webpage:

•   You can use the font family property to adjust the face of your selected font.

•   You can use the font style property to make your fonts either oblique or italic.

•   You can use the font variant property to include the "small caps" effect in your fonts.

•   You can use the font weight property to decrease or increase how light or bold your fonts are displayed.

•   You can use the font size property to decrease or increase the sizes of your fonts.

•   You can use the font property to define a combination of the font properties above.

How to Define the Font Family

Here is an example on how you can define the font family of a specific element. As value of the property, you can use any of the font family names available:

This message is displayed either in calibri, arial or the default serif font. It will depend on the existing fonts in your system.

How to Define the Font Style

Here is an example on how you can define the font style of a specific element. The values that you can use are oblique, italic or normal.

This message is displayed in oblique style.

How to Define the Font Variant

Here is an example on how you define the font variant of a specific element. The values that you can use are small-caps or normal.

This message is displayed in normal font variant.

How to Define the Font Weight

Here is an example on how you can define the font weight of a specific element. With this property, you will be able to define how bold you want your fonts to be. The values that you can use are bold, normal, lighter, bolder, 100, 200, 300, 400, 500, 600, 700, 800, and 900.

The font is displayed with normal font weight.

The font is displayed with lighter font weight.

The font is displayed with 800 font weight.

How to Define the Font Size

Here is an example on how you can define the font size of a specific element. With this property, you will be able to control the font sizes in your webpage. The values that you can use include small, medium, large, x-small, xx-small, xx-large, x-large, larger, smaller, size in % or size in pixels.

The font is displayed with 18 pixels font size.

```
<p style="font-size:large;">
```

The font is displayed with large font size.

```
</p>
```

```
<p style="font-size:larger;">
```

The font is displayed with larger font size.

```
</p>
```

How to Define the Font Size Adjust

Here is an example on how you can define the font size adjust of a specific element. With this property, you will be able to adjust the x-height in order to make the legibility of your fonts better. The values that you can use include any number.

```
<p style="font-size-adjust:0.75;">
```

The font is displayed with 0.75 font size adjust value.

```
</p>
```

How to Define the Font Stretch

Here is an example on how you can define the font stretch of a specific element. With this property, you can allow the computer of your webpage readers to have a condensed or expanded version of the font you have defined in your elements. The values that you can use include normal, narrower, wider, condensed, extra-condensed, semi-condensed, ultra-condensed, semi-expanded, ultra-expanded, expanded and extra-expanded

```
<p style="font-stretch:ultra-condensed;">
```

If this does not seem to work, it is probably that the computer you are using does not have an expanded or condensed version of the font that was used.

```
</p>
```

How to Use the Shorthand Property

You can utilize the font property to define the font properties all at the same time.

Example:

This applies all of the defined properties on the text all at the same time.

Conclusion

Thank you again for purchasing this book!

I hope this book was able to help you to understand the basic CSS styling rules.

The next step is to apply what you have just learned in your own webpage.

Finally, if you enjoyed this book, please take the time to share your thoughts and post a review on Amazon. We do our best to reach out to readers and provide the best value we can. Your positive review will help us achieve that. It'd be greatly appreciated!

Thank you and good luck!

Check Out My Other Books

Below you'll find some of my other popular books that are popular on Amazon and Kindle as well. Simply click on the links below to check them out. Alternatively, you can visit my author page on Amazon to see other work done by me.

Android Programming in a Day

Python Programming in a Day

C Programming Success in a Day

C Programming Professional Made Easy

JavaScript Programming Made Easy

PHP Programming Professional Made Easy

C ++ Programming Success in a Day

Windows 8 Tips for Beginners

HTML Professional Programming Made Easy

If the links do not work, for whatever reason, you can simply search for these titles on the Amazon website to find them.